I0115139

THE
JIMMY JONES
SKANDAL

A Bedtime Story
for Grown-Ups
only!

Copyright © Donovan O'Malley 2010

The right of Donovan O'Malley to be identified as the
author of this work has been asserted by him in
accordance with the Copyright, Designs
and Patent's Act of 1988.

All rights reserved.
Apart from any use permitted by UK copyright law no
part of this publication may be reproduced, stored in
a retrieval system, or transmitted, in any form or by
any means without the prior written permission of the
publisher, nor be otherwise circulated in any form of
binding or cover other than in which it is published and
without a similar condition being imposed on the
subsequent purchaser.

ISBN 978-91-979188-3-1

Cover Design by Leif Sodergren

With special thanks to Gary Wadas

WRITTEN AND ILLUSTRATED BY
DONOVAN O'MALLEY

THE
JIMMY JONES
SKANDAL

A BEDTIME STORY
FOR GROWN-UPS
ONLY!

LEMONGULCHBOOKS
www.lemongulchbooks.com

Jimmy Jones

was a normal, carefree,
Full of vim and vinegar little boy...

He played Cowboys and Indians,

He **hated** to take a bath...

...AND
LOVED SWEETS !

The only difference
between Jimmy and
any other healthy, adjusted,

child of five

WAS...

He had a forty-year-old
Mistress!!!

This, of course, posed problems
peculiar for a child of his age,

such as...

Buying cocktails for his beloved who drank like a fish and preferred the most expensive and exotic drinks -- Singapore Slings and Sloe-Gin Fizzes and Zombies.

Obviously, he couldn't convince the barman that he was of legal age...so she had to write a note each time she wished to imbibe... and it was often.

Very often!!!

And
the cigarette girl
would only pat him on the
head

and pinch his little
pink cheek...

...so he had to buy cigarettes
from a machine that was
ten minutes away...

And hard to reach
when he got there!!!

This was extremely annoying because
his mistress smoked her cigarettes
only halfway down!

These, however, were
minor problems!!

Nothing was more humiliating than
the look on the face of
the pharmacist the day Jimmy
attempted to purchase
another necessity
for his precocious romantic
endeavors!

Jimmy's friends told him how silly and extravagant they thought his affair to be!

The price of only one of her exotic cocktails could keep them all

in sweets for a week!

But Jimmy, whose **heart**
belonged to his forty-year-old
paramour, would have none of it...

"Honey that is aged" he would say with

a childlike grin, "is the finest honey"

UNTIL...

LOLA MAY ANDERSON
CAME TO TOWN!!!

Lola May was not what one could call exceptionally pretty nor was her taste in clothes particularly sophisticated.

She was not seductive as her strict middle-class upbringing prevented her competing along the same sinewy lines as Jimmy's aging good-time-gal.

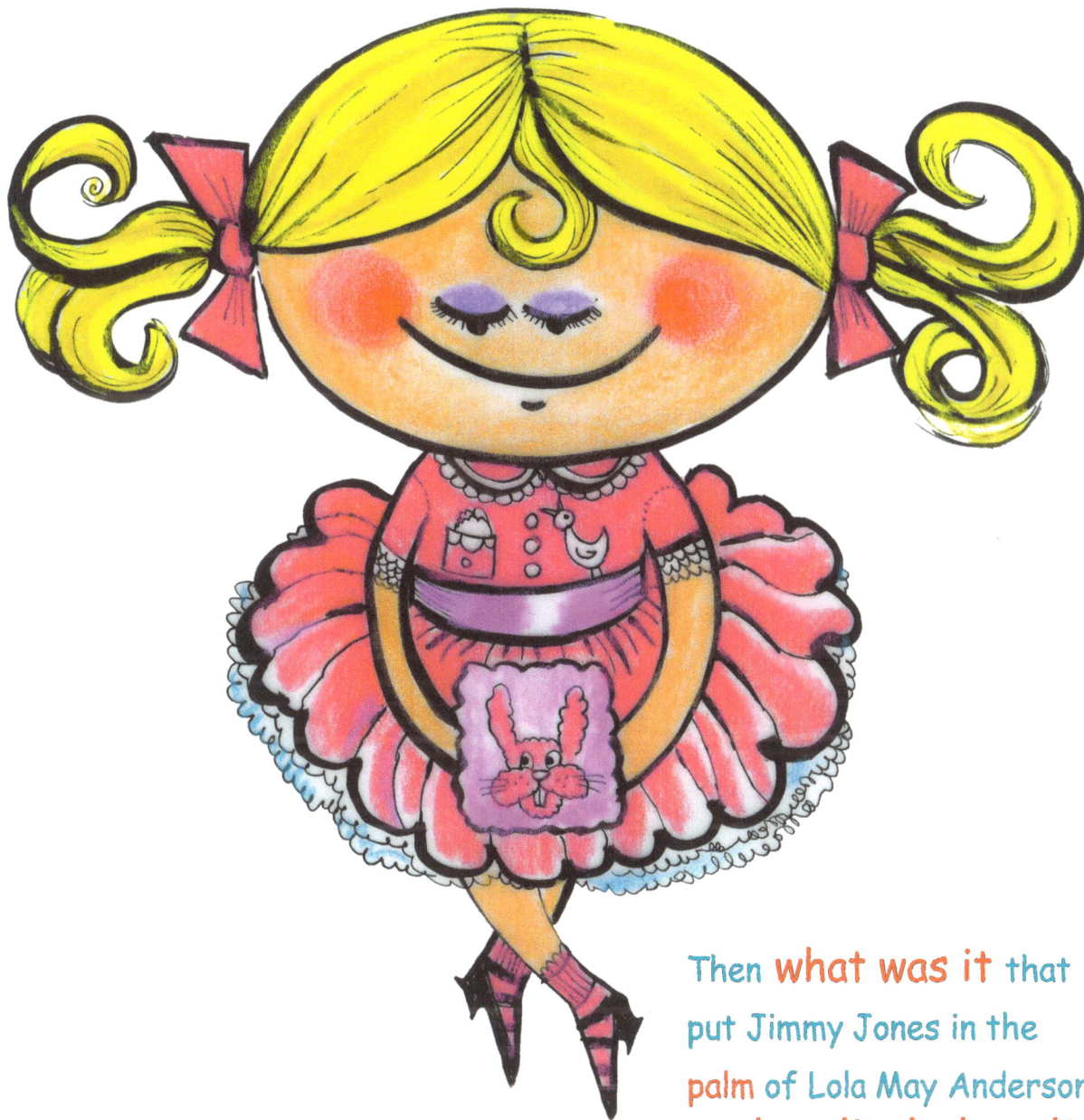

Then what was it that
put Jimmy Jones in the
palm of Lola May Anderson's
pudgy, little hand?!

Jimmy's mistress
immediately sensed
something untoward....
something very unfair...
became so nervous she SHED HAIR ....

...and so upset that she was
forced to use BOTH HANDS to
take out a cigarette...and she now
smoked them

all the way down
to the filters!

She began to drink
even more than before!

and was near complete

nervous collapse !

when she looked
out her window
and saw...

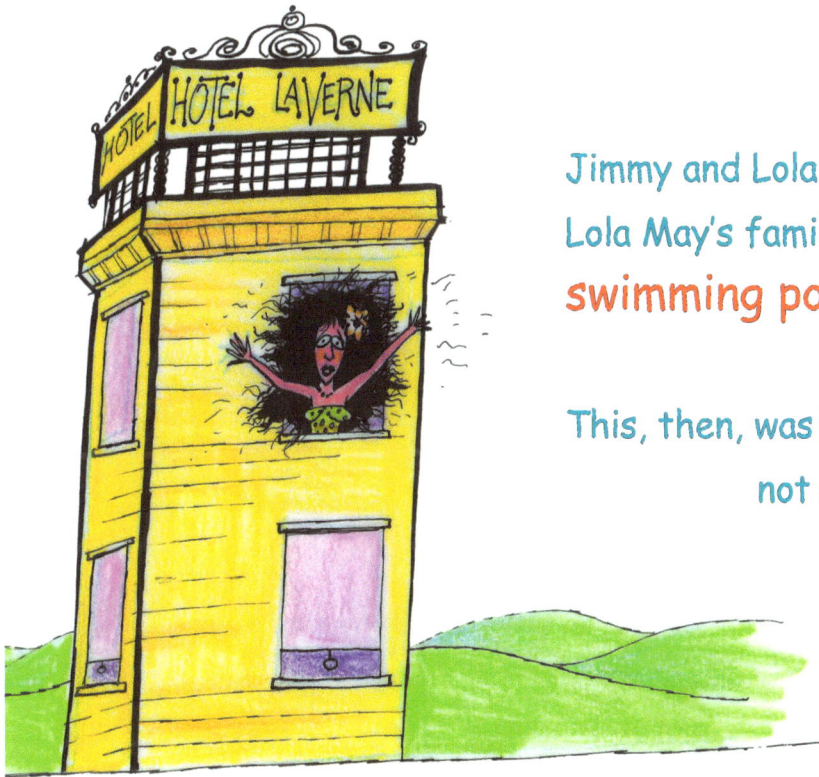

Jimmy and Lola May Anderson in
Lola May's family
swimming pool!!

This, then, was Lola May's
not so hidden
attraction!

The poor woman went instantly
to the nearest bar to ponder
her predicament.
Lola May, she strongly felt, was
pinching Jimmy under the water!

She considered poisoning Lola May's sweets or
putting Piranha fish in Lola May's family's
swimming pool.

But, being an honest paramour
she decided to present her problem
forthrightly to Lola May,
woman-to-girl.
So, the next day...

she hurried to the park

where Jimmy and his little friends
were often to be found.

There, she knew she would find
Lola May and would
throw herself
on the child's mercy.

Lola May was playing marbles with Jimmy
and **winning!**

Before she poured out her secret heart
to the child she required
bargaining power...

so she scurried off to the sweet shops and
bought dozens of jelly beans and licorice sticks
and cookies as well as three
particularly appealing cupcakes

Lola May Anderson
was easily swayed
by this plethora of sweeties,
But held out for the last jelly-bean
before she gave her solemn word

never to see
Jimmy again.

She was bored with Jimmy
and anyway had already
won all his marbles.

Her mission
accomplished...

the failing, though
still genial courtesan

combed her hair,
freshened her
lavish makeup...

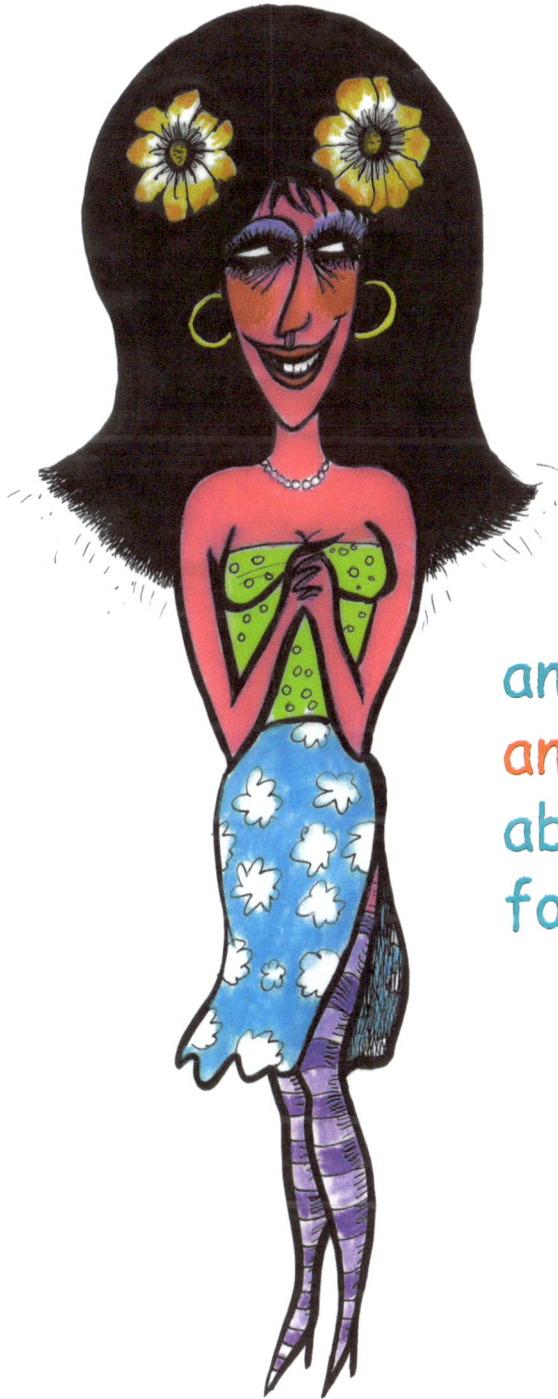

and looked
anxiously
about
for Jimmy...

but he was
nowhere
to be found !!!

He had run away with

the cigarette girl

with whom he had been

carrying-on all along !!!!!!

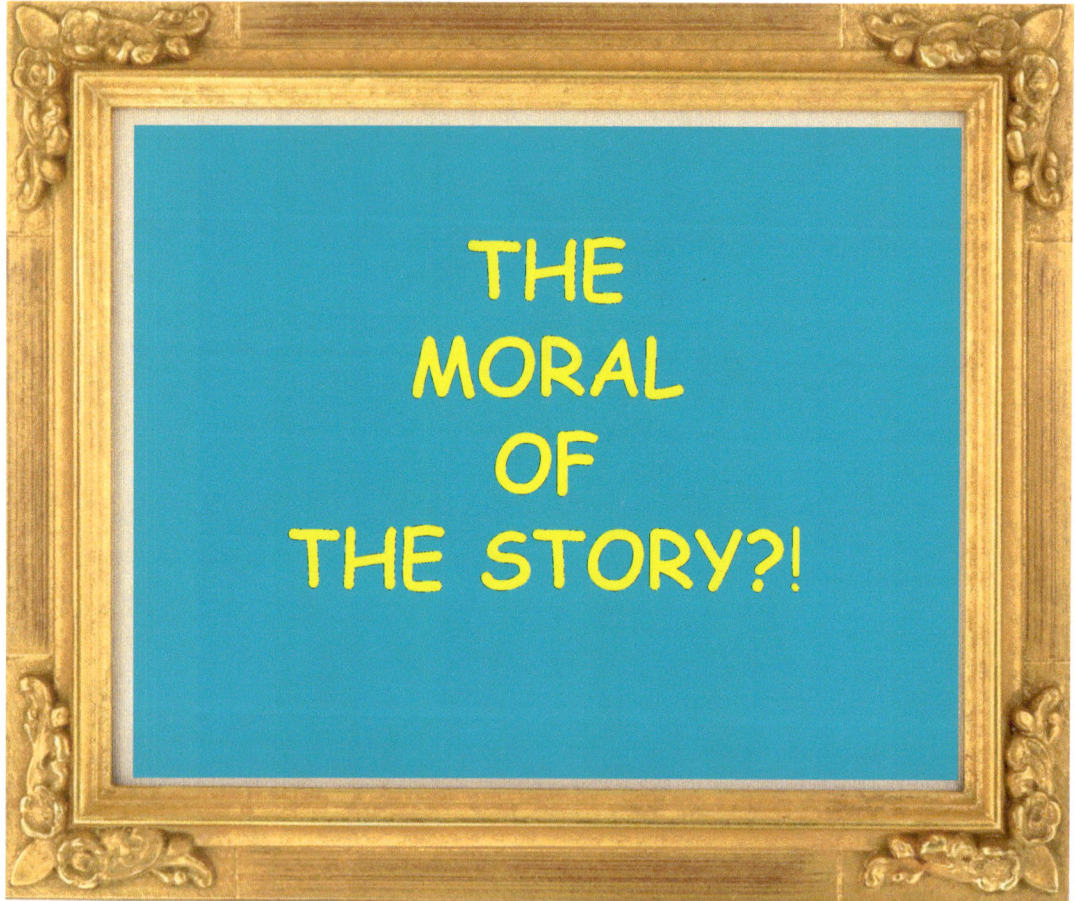

THE
MORAL
OF
THE STORY?!

Also by Donovan O'Malley

LEMON GULCH
New Edition

A darkly comic moral tale.
12-year-old over-grown precocious
misfit Danny, narrates his
surprising adventures
in his search for acceptance
in "a uncaring world".

OUR YANK
A comic novel.
An American student comes of age
in Oxford during the Cuban
Missile Crisis of 1962.
Seventeen-year old Andy has left
sunny California to study in
rainy Oxford against
the backdrop of a possible
nuclear war over Russian
missiles in Cuba.

THE IMPORTANCE
OF HAVING SPUNK
A lesbian couple's comic search
for the perfect donor in the
Scandinavian wilderness.
A Comic Novel with a twist
to the battle of the sexes,
and a nod to Oscar Wilde

www.ingramcontent.com/pod-product-compliance
Lightning Source LLC
Chambersburg PA
CBHW060831270326
41933CB00002B/51